Judith Simon Prager, PhD

Owie Cadabra's

Verbal First Aid™ for Kids

A somewhat magical way to help
heal yourself and your friends.

Illustrations by David Hudnut

The author of this book does not dispense medical advice or prescribe the use of any techniques as forms of treatment for physical or medical problems without the advice of a physician, either directly or indirectly. The intent of the author is only to offer information of a general nature to help you in your quest for emotional and spiritual well-being. In the event you use any of the information in this book for yourself, which is your constitutional right, the author and the publisher assume no responsibility for your actions.

Text copyright ©2010 by Judith Simon Prager
www.verbalfirstaidforkids.com

Illustrated by David Hudnut
Illustrations copyright ©2010 by David Hudnut
Design by Rochelle Hampton

ISBN 1453648216
EAN-13–9781453648216

For
Jack, Tanner, Maddie, Izzie,
and all the world's children.

If you want happiness for a lifetime—
help the next generation.

Thanks to Elizabeth Guilliams for magnetizing
everyone involved in making this project a reality.

Once upon a time there was a boy who fell off his bike and got an owie.

Did that ever happen to you?

Did that ever happen to your friend?

Did you want to go over to your friend and make it all better?

Well, this boy named Oliver fell down and Oliver's father came over to see what was happening.

"Oh, Oliver," his Dad said, "you're bleeding!"

And so he was—
his knee was bleeding.

6

That can be scary.

It can make your heart beat faster,
or maybe make your belly feel funny,
or your hands feel sweaty,
or your throat feel like you want
to swallow hard.

Or it might even make tears come
to your eyes.

You know why you feel funny
when you're scared?
Because your body is listening.

Your body is listening to what you're
thinking or feeling!

And when we feel afraid, we
sometimes have all those other
feelings in our bodies, too.

Well, maybe not yours, not now...but Oliver
felt that when he looked at his knee.

And his Dad didn't quite know what to say.

Then, just sort of out of nowhere in
a shining bubble that burst,

a smiling person appeared.

Oliver was so surprised, he stopped crying
and asked, "Who are you?"

"They call me...Owie-Cadabra," she said.

"I've heard of Abracadabra for magic," said
Oliver's friend Emily.

"Right. And I'm magic for owies," said
Owie-Cadabra..

"I know the magic words that help start your healing from the inside," said Owie-Cadabra.

"From the inside?" asked Oliver's Dad.

Owie-Cadabra smiled. "Oliver's body knows how to heal itself," she said. "It always has."

She turned to Oliver, "Remember the last time you had a cut and put a bandage on it? And when you took the bandage off a few days later, the cut was..."

"Gone!" said Oliver.

"Yeah," said Oliver's friend Miguel, "but was that from the inside?!"

"Of course," said Owie-Cadabra, "only your body could knit itself back together in that wonderful way!"

15

"What magic words?" Emily said.

Owie-Cadabra looked at Emily with a smile.
"Ah, you were listening!"

"Yeah. What magic words?
And how can they make it better?"

"Well that's two questions,"
said Owie-Cadabra:
"Let's help Oliver here and see."

"Okay Oliver, so if I were your friend Emily,
and Oliver's Daddy weren't nearby, the first
thing I'd say is "I'm right here." And "I'll stay
with you and I'll send someone to get help."

"How does that make things better?"
asked Emily.

16

17

"Well," Owie-Cadabra asked Oliver,
"how would you feel if you fell down...
and no one was around?"

"Scared," said Oliver.

"Yes. But if a friend came by and said,
'Oh, if you need help, I'm right here,'
how would you feel?"

"A little better," said Oliver.

"In fact," said Owie-Cadabra, "your body
would feel a little better, too.
Because inside your body are chemicals,
like drops of different kinds of energy.
Some of them make you feel jumpy and
nervous, and others make you feel calm.
And when you're scared,
which ones do you think you feel?"

"Nervous and um...jumpy?" asked Oliver.

Owie-Cadabra nodded.

Then Emily got a bright idea:
"But when someone makes you feel safer,
you feel calm!" she said.

Owie-Cadabra beamed at her.
"Right!" she said. "And when you feel calm,
drops of different chemicals go through
your body like good medicine that
start the healing so you can start
feeling and getting better."

20

Band-
ages

22

"So that's it?" said Emily. "That's **all**?!"

Owie-Cadabra started pulling all kinds of things out of her magic sleeves.

Snow, bandages, magic glasses to see the future when it's "all better," a sink faucet...

"Oh, no," she said, "there's lots more.
Like, watch this. Oliver, can you imagine
that you had a faucet there, where
your knee is bleeding?"

Owie-Cadabra put her little faucet on
Oliver's knee. "The blood is there to
clean the cut, and when it's cleaned,
can you imagine turning it off so the
bleeding stops? Like a tap in the sink
when you turn off the water?"

Oliver thought about it.
"Yeah...maybe."

"And while he's doing that," Owie-Cadabra said,
turning to Oliver's friend Sophie,
"you could ask him to check his arm, or his nose
to see if everything else is all right.
Go ahead," she said to Sophie, "ask him."

Sophie pointed to Oliver's nose and asked
"How's your nose, Oliver?"

Oliver smiled and laughed.

"That's right," Owie-Cadabra said.
"And you," she said to Miguel,
"ask him how his elbow is."

"How's your elbow, Oliver?" said Miguel.

Oliver thought about it, wondering.

"When he's not thinking about his knee,"
Owie-Cadabra said,
"it doesn't bother him so much."

"Oh, yeah, my knee," said Oliver.
He'd forgotten all about his knee!

"How's the faucet doing?"
asked Owie-Cadabra.

"Hmmmm....It stopped bleeding."

"Yes, that can happen,"
said Owie-Cadabra.

29

"Oliver looks pretty good now.
But what if he were really hurt and crying?
You know what we could say to him?"

"What?"
everybody, even Oliver's Dad, asked.

Owie-Cadabra pulled a TV set
out of her sleeve.
"We could ask him, how would your favorite
superhero fix it if that happened to him?"

"He'd use his superpowers to fix it up!"
Oliver shouted out.

"Yeah!" said Sophie.

"Can you picture that?"
Owie-Cadabra asked. "How's that feel?"

"Funny," Oliver said. "Better."

"When your mind pictures something," Owie-Cadabra said, "your body may do it. You have white blood cells in your body that are like calling 911 to come to the rescue.

32

If you picture the white blood cells like, oh maybe fire fighters or the police coming to help, your body goes right into action to fix things up. Your body is already working on making it better. Right as soon as it happened, your body called a 'red alert' and your white blood cells were sent down to fight the 'bugs.' One kind of white blood cell is chasing them away, others are making a scab, which is like your body's own bandage and making new skin."

"I've heard about that," said Sophie's Mom.

Did you ever burn yourself in hot
water or in the flame of a candle or
on something hot on the stove?"
Owie-Cadabra asked the kids.

"I did once," said Sophie holding up her
hand and remembering how it hurt.

"Of course you want to get a grown up
to help, but here's what YOU can do:
Inside your mind, picture the part that was
burned packed in cool, cool snow. Feel it!"
Owie pulled some more snow
out of her pocket and sprinkled it on
all of them, so they giggled.

"You know why that helps?
Because your body is listening
to your thoughts," Owie-Cadabra said.

"If you're thinking that your body will heal
itself, your brain sends your body those
wonderful tiny chemicals inside you that
have messages that tell it to repair itself."

"Like little fire fighters," said Oliver.

"Like superheroes," said Miguel.

"Like angels?" said Emily.

"Like whatever good thing you can imagine,"
said Owie-Cadabra.

"And if you think about some place you'd like
to be or someone who makes you happy,
your body also sends the chemicals that
can start the healing."

"Like swimming or sledding?" said Oliver.

"Or my puppy?" asked Sophie.

"Yes!" said Owie-Cadabra.
"What you're thinking when you're hurt or upset affects how your body feels and how quickly it can get better. How about that!"

"Your body likes to heal itself.
It likes to get better.
And when you're thinking about it getting
better, it likes to do it even more."

Owie-Cadabra pulled a pair of glasses
from her sleeve. "And you can put on these
make-believe magic glasses and picture
what it will be like when you're all better—
good as new—and that
makes it better faster, too."

Oliver put the glasses on and pictured
himself running around just fine.
"I can see myself all better!" he said.

"And one more thing," said Owie-Cadabra. "Whenever you're upset, just tell yourself or your friend to remember to breathe!

"If you pretend you're blowing out a birthday candle, and then take in a nice deep breath, your body will say a big thank you for that!"

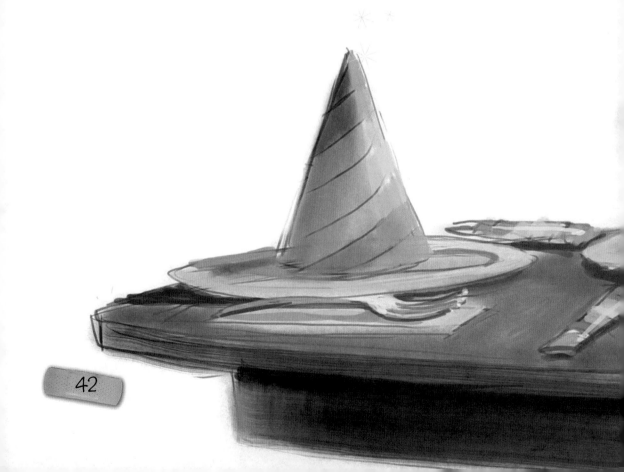

Oliver's Dad and Sophie's Mom had been
listening to all this and they smiled.
"So whenever one of our friends gets hurt,
we can remind them of all these ways
to start the healing from the inside!"
Oliver's Dad said.

"Yes, and you know what else?"
Owie-Cadabra asked. "You can tell yourself
the very same things. Your thoughts send
messages to your body, so your thoughts
and words can help the healing from the—"

"Inside!" said Oliver.

"Can everybody do that?"
asked Owie-Cadabra.

"Yes!"
they all said together.

"Thanks a lot, Owie-Cadabra!"
the kids shouted, as she floated
away waving.

46

Then Oliver's Dad said, "Let's go home and clean that cut and put on a bandage. Now we know just what to picture to help your body make it all better."

Oliver's friends all went off to play.
And as Emily ran towards the swings,
she tripped and fell down.

"Owwwch!" she said. "I think I'm hurt."
She looked around, and no one was there.

She looked at her hands and they were
bleeding...and she started to feel scared.

And then she thought to herself, "Hmm.
Well, what would Owie-Cadabra say?"

And she heard in her head,
"Your body knows how to heal itself...."

53

From across the playground Sophie ran
towards Emily as she called to Miguel,
"Go get her Mom!"

Sophie came to Emily's side, knelt
down next to her and said,
"It's all right, Emily. I'm right here."

And Emily felt safe and okay.

Here are some Owie-Cadabra magic words you can say to your friends or yourself to make it "all better."

♥ "Your body knows how to heal itself! Remember the last time that you had an owie and in a few days when you took the bandage off, the owie was gone."

♥ "How would you favorite superhero or character fix it? Can you imagine or pretend that?"

♥ "Picture a faucet and turn off the bleeding when I count to five."

♥ "Imagine telling your friends how brave you were."

♥ If you remember another friend who had a fall like that, you could say, "My friend Jayden fell down in the playground last week, and he's running around now good as new..."

♥ "Remember a time when you felt happy or a place you love to be." It will send chemicals like little fire fighters to help the healing.

♥ "Picture it with snow all around it while we get Mom to help." It will make it numb and more comfortable.

♥ "Use imaginary glasses to picture how it will be when you're all better and playing again!"

♥ If you bump your arm, check out your toe. If you bump your toe, check out your elbow.

♥ Whenever you take medicine or put medicine on a cut or burn, imagine how much it will help.

♥ And don't forget to...

"Breathe!"

Owie-Cadabra's
Verbal First Aid Song

If your friend's hurt or afraid
Use Owie-Cadabra's Verbal First Aid
Say "I'm right here," and "breathe with me,"
It's as easy as one, two, three.

If an owie makes you cry
Remember this healing lullaby
"Your body knows just what to do
To heal the cut as good as new."

When you're scared or feeling sick
Think of a super hero quick
What would they do, then imagine it too
With Verbal First Aid, it's up to you.

Call Owie-Cadabra and you'll know what to say
And heal from inside the Verbal First Aid way!
Owie-Cadabra!

A note to moms and dads about
Verbal First Aid

ccidents and owies happen. And when our kids are injured, we sometimes get very upset ourselves, and we say things like "Oh, no! My poor baby! Does it hurt a lot? It looks bad." And that can frighten them, because they turn to you to see how serious it is.

Or, because we want it to go away quickly, we may say, "You're all right. It's nothing." And when we do, our children may feel that we're dismissing their feelings and they may begin to dismiss their own feelings, too.

But with Verbal First Aid, you can actually physically and emotionally set a course for recovery that can put healing thoughts into your children's minds when they need them most, thoughts that help them know how to start the healing themselves. Your words and the way you say them can mean the difference between panic and calm, pain and comfort, even how and whether healing happens.

Once you know the science behind this, the ways to gain the special rapport that makes this so effective, and how you can affect not only how the child heals in the moment, but how he or she remembers the incident in the future, you'll be able to give your children the tools that provide a sense of their own inner healing mastery for life.

It's all in the book *Verbal First Aid: Help Your Kids Heal From Fear and Pain—And Come Out Strong,* by Judith Simon Prager, PhD and Judith Acosta, LISW, Berkley Books, 2010.

Your kids can learn lots more about it, hear Owie's songs and other special music, and experience guided imagery for changing sad or mad to glad at: www.verbalfirstaidforkids.com.

You can learn about me and my work at: www.judithprager.com.

To learn more about the illustrator, David Hudnut, visit his website at: www.hudnutart.com.

"A PROFOUND PRESCRIPTION FOR NURTURING OUR CHILDREN."
—Bruce H. Lipton, PhD, bestselling author of *The Biology of Belief*

Verbal First Aid

Help Your Kids Heal from Fear and Pain— and Come Out Strong

JUDITH SIMON PRAGER, PhD
and JUDITH ACOSTA, LCSW, CHT
authors of *The Worst Is Over*

About the Author

J udith Simon Prager, PhD is a hypnotherapist with a private practice in Los Angeles, CA. She teaches in the UCLA Ext. Writers' Program with her husband, Harry Youtt, where they were recognized as "Outstanding Instructors" of 2004.

Co-author with Judith Acosta of *The Worst Is Over: What To Say When Every Moment Counts*, named "The 'bible' for crisis communications," by *The International Journal of Emergency Medicine*, and co-author of *Verbal First Aid: Help Your Kids Heal From Fear and Pain—And Come Out Strong*, she has trained doctors, nurses, and first responders in the Verbal First Aid protocol at medical centers across the United States, in England, and in China after the devastating 2008 earthquake.

Mother of two, step-mother of two, and grandmother of four wonderful children, she wrote this book in the hopes that all children learn how to speak to themselves and each other in a way that is self-healing and empowering, helping themselves and blessing the future in the process.

About the Illustrator

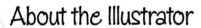

David Hudnut is a raconteur to the highest degree. Having for a time served as the White Chocolatier (sans musket), fourth member of Dumas' fabled band of fanciful foilers, he has traveled the world in search of wrongs to be righted.

Since retiring his épée, and taking seriously that rusty old catch phrase, took up the pen, not with the intention of wielding the mightier weaponry of ideas, but of squiggling lines that metaphorically evoke reality via the visual poetry of drawing. But always one to give respect where it is due, he has long maintained, that indeed, a word is worth 1,000 pictures. And during his tenure as artist, has thus produced the equivalent of 8 or 9 words.

Notable works elaborated and enhanced by his synesthetic scribbling include the instant classic *Kittens With No Mittens, Iron Mandible 2, and Frankenstein's Hamster.* David lives in the Pacific Northwest with the love of his life Rochelle.

63

Made in the USA
Middletown, DE
05 December 2021

54365021R00040